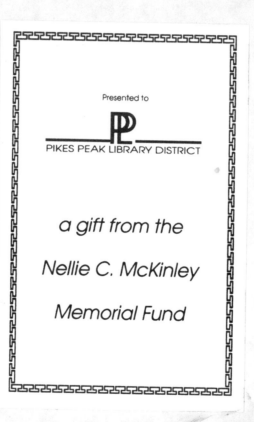

A ROOKIE BIOGRAPHY

FRANCES HODGSON BURNETT

Author of The Secret Garden

By Carol Greene

CHILDRENS PRESS ®

CHICAGO

Frances Hodgson Burnett (1849-1924)

Library of Congress Cataloging-in-Publication Data

Greene, Carol.
    Frances Hodgson Burnett: author of *The secret garden* / by Carol
Greene.
        p.   cm. — (A Rookie biography)
    Includes index.
    ISBN 0-516-04268-8
    1. Burnett, Frances Hodgson, 1849-1924—Biography—Juvenile
literature. 2. Authors, American—20th century—Biography—Juvenile
literature. 3. Children's stories—Authorship—Juvenile literature.
[1. Burnett, Frances Hodgson, 1849-1924. 2. Authors, American.
3. Women—Biography.] I. Title. II. Series: Greene, Carol. Rookie
biography.
PS1216.G74   1995
813'.4–dc20
    [B]   94-37500
                                                              CIP
                                                               AC

Frances Hodgson Burnett
was a real person.
She was born in 1849
and died in 1924.
Frances wrote many books.
But her best one,
The Secret Garden,
was for children.
This is her story.

TABLE OF CONTENTS

Manchester, England, in 1885

Chapter 1

Gardens and Stories

Manchester, England, was
a dark, dirty city
when Frances Hodgson
was a little girl.
But behind her house
grew a garden.

"The Back Garden was always
full of beautiful wonders,"
she wrote years later.

The Hodgson family left that house
when Frances was six.
But in her mind,
she saw the garden
for the rest of her life.

Frances' father was dead.
Her mother had to run
the family's hardware business
and care for her five children.
There wasn't much money.
But the children went to school.

Frances had learned to read
when she was only three.
She made up stories too.
She and her doll acted
them out on the nursery couch.

Her big brothers teased her
about those stories.
But Frances ignored them.

Girls at Frances' school
took turns reading aloud.
One day, Frances didn't read.
She told a story of her own.
It was about the adventures
of a beautiful lady.

The other girls loved it.
After that, they made
Frances tell stories every day.
Soon she began to
write her stories down.

Frances still thought
about gardens, too.
Her house didn't have one.
But nearby stood
an old empty house.

Across the back
stretched a brick wall.
In it was a green door.
Did a beautiful garden
lie behind that door?

One day, Frances found
the door unlocked.
She pushed it open
and there lay a garden,
full of trash and weeds.

But in Frances' mind,
the weeds became roses
and lilies and violets.
The trash became fountains.
Frances never forgot
her pretend garden either.

As time passed, the Hodgsons
had less and less money.
They couldn't buy paper.
So Frances wrote her stories
on old shopping lists.
Mrs. Hodgson worried all the time.

Then Mrs. Hodgson's brother
wrote from his home
in the United States.
Why didn't the Hodgsons
move over there too?
He'd help them find jobs.

Frances at about age 16

So, when Frances was 16,
she and her family
set off for America.

Knoxville, Tennessee, about the time Frances lived there

Chapter 2

A Young Writer

~~~~~~

Frances' new home was
in Knoxville, Tennessee.
Her brothers, John and Herbert,
soon found jobs.

But the family was still poor.
For a while, they lived
in a log cabin.
Sometimes they were hungry.

Frances didn't mind.
She had woods to roam in,
like a huge, wild garden.
At night, she could curl up
with her kitten and write.

Her brothers still made
fun of her stories.
They called them "bosh."
But her sisters, Edith
and Edwina, liked them.

One day, Frances had an idea.
Maybe she could sell
her stories to magazines!
But she had no money
for paper or stamps.

So the next day, Frances
and her sisters picked
wild grapes in the woods.
They sold them at the market
and Frances bought her
paper and stamps.

The first magazine didn't
want Frances' story.
But the second one did.
It wanted *two* stories.
Soon Frances had a check
for thirty-five dollars.

She showed it to Herbert.

"Well, by Jove!" he said.
He never called Frances'
stories "bosh" again.

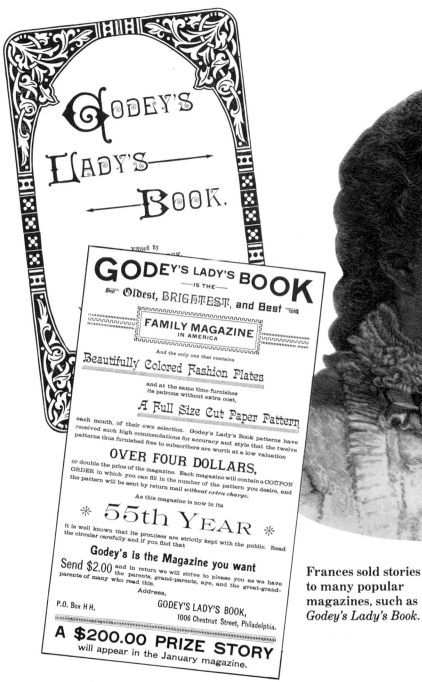

Frances sold stories
to many popular
magazines, such as
Godey's Lady's Book.

She was a real writer now.

And she was only 18.

VOL. XXI. N° 5   MAY, 1897   PRICE 25 CENTS

SCRIBNER'S MAGAZINE

CHARLES SCRIBNER'S SONS

**Frances sold stories
to *Scribner's Magazine*,
where Richard Watson Gilder
(right) was her editor.**

Chapter 3

Little Lord Fauntleroy

Soon Frances earned enough
to help her whole family.
Five or six stories came out
each month in ladies' magazines.

The Hodgsons moved
to a big brick house
and began to have fun.
They gave parties, made music,
and went for boat rides.

Frances at about age 21

When Frances was 21,
her mother died.
Her brothers had moved away.
She was head of the family.

A young doctor, Swan Burnett,
wanted to marry Frances.
She said no.
Swan was a good friend,
but she didn't love him.

Swan wouldn't give up.
So Frances made a promise.
She would travel to England.
Then, when she got back,
she would marry him.

Frances was
24 years old
when she married
Swan Burnett.

Frances was
gone a year.
But Swan waited.
They were
married in 1873.
In 1874, Frances
had a little boy,
Lionel.

Still she kept writing.
Her stories got better
and she earned more money.
When Swan wanted to study
in Paris, France,
Frances paid the way.

Paris, France, about 1890

Paris was beautiful,
but Frances couldn't enjoy it.
She was too busy writing
so her family could eat.

The Burnetts lived in this neighborhood in Washington, D.C.

In 1876, Frances had
another little boy, Vivian.
Soon the family moved
to Washington, D.C.

There Frances turned
a long story into a
book for adults.
It did so well that
she wrote more books.

By then, Frances was famous.
She could hire people to help
care for her home and children.
That was good, because
she had to travel a lot.

Frances' boys called her "Dearest."
They missed her sometimes.
But they were healthy and happy.
Swan and Frances weren't happy.
They shouldn't have married.
Frances knew that.

One day, Vivian said,
"Why don't you write
some books that little boys
would like to read?"

So Frances wrote
Little Lord Fauntleroy.
It is the story of Cedric,
an American boy who becomes
a "little lord" in England.

Cedric isn't
a sissy. But
he has long
curls and
wears velvet
suits with
lace collars.

This illustration from *Little Lord Fauntleroy*
shows Cedric in his velvet and lace.

Little Lord Fauntleroy in England

Boys liked the book.
But then their mothers
wanted to dress *them*
in velvet and lace.
The boys hated that.

Little Lord Fauntleroy
did very well.
Soon it was number one
on the best-seller list.

A movie was made of *Little Lord Fauntleroy*. It starred Mary Pickford as Cedric.

Right: Illustrations from
A Little Princess.
Above: Frances in 1890

Chapter 4

Struggles

In 1888, Frances wrote
another children's book.
This time the hero was a girl.
Later, Frances called this story
A Little Princess.
It did well too.

Frances liked to visit Europe.
Sometimes she took her boys.
But in 1890, their trip was sad.
Lionel had tuberculosis.
Many people died of
that disease in those days.

After Lionel died,
Frances kept this
statue of him
in her house.

Frances hoped doctors in Europe
could help Lionel.
But they couldn't.
He died in Paris at age 16.

Friends everywhere tried
to comfort Frances.
But for a long time,
she wanted to die too.

Frances kept busy
helping poor children.
She remembered how
it felt to be poor.
Many of her stories were
about poor people.

Writing helped Frances
feel better too.
Then she and Swan were divorced.
Divorce was unusual
at that time, but they
were just too unhappy together.

Old-fashioned roses like these bloomed in Frances'
English garden. The English robin (inset) is smaller and
more brightly colored than the robin of North America.

Frances found herself a house
in the country in England.
It had gardens with brick walls.
She filled one garden with roses
and that was where she wrote.

In this garden lived
a small robin.
He became Frances' friend.
He flew to meet her,
ate from her hand,
and sat on her shoulder.

In 1900, Frances married
a man named Stephen Townesend.
That was a mistake.
He was too bossy.
The marriage didn't last long.

Frances in the early 1900s

In 1904, Frances became
a citizen of the United States.
She decided to build herself
a home on Long Island.
Of course, it would have gardens.

Chapter 5

The Secret Garden

Frances' new home
was big and beautiful.
So were its gardens.
But soon Frances was thinking
about another garden.

**Roses and hollyhocks
bloomed in the garden
of Frances' home
on Long Island.**

This garden would
bloom in a book.
She would make it from all
the gardens she remembered—

the Back Garden,
full of wonders;
the poor, weedy garden
behind the green door;
and the rose garden with
its friendly little robin.

The Secret Garden

By Frances Hodgson Burnett
Illustrated by Tasha Tudor

In her mind, Frances
put them all together
and wrote
The Secret Garden.

In this illustration from the book, Mary explores the secret garden.

In the book, an unhappy girl,
Mary, goes to live in a mansion.
There, a friendly robin
helps her find a secret garden.
But everything in it looks dead.

Together, Mary and two boys
make the garden live again.
And as they do, they find
new lives for themselves.

Frances wrote more books
after *The Secret Garden*.
But she never felt well.

Frances continued to write books as well as stories for magazines. In *The Century Monthly Magazine*, one of her stories is illustrated on the cover.

Frances had worked hard
for many years and
her body was tired.

At last, she had to stay in bed.
But she could see the flowers
in her garden outside.
So Frances lay there and
wrote and was happy.

All her life,
Frances loved
books and
writing.

Frances Hodgson Burnett
died in her home
on October 29, 1924.
She was 74 years old.

Important Dates

1849   November 24—Born in Manchester, England, to Eliza and Edwin Hodgson

1865   Moved to Knoxville, Tennessee

1868   Published first story, "Hearts and Diamonds," in *Godey's Lady's Book*

1873   Married Swan Burnett

1874   Son Lionel born

1876   Son Vivian born

1886   *Little Lord Fauntleroy* published

1890   Lionel died

1898   Divorced Swan Burnett

1908   Built home on Long Island, New York

1911   *The Secret Garden* published

1924   October 29—Died at home on Long Island

INDEX

Page numbers in boldface type indicate illustrations.

PHOTO CREDITS

ABOUT THE AUTHOR

Carol Greene has degrees in English literature and musicology. She has worked in international exchange programs, as an editor, and as a teacher of writing. She now lives in Webster Groves, Missouri, and writes full-time. She has published more than 100 books, including those in the Childrens Press Rookie Biographies series.

ABOUT THE ILLUSTRATOR

Of Cajun origins, Steven Gaston Dobson was born and raised in New Orleans, Louisiana. He attended art school in the city and worked as a newspaper artist on the *New Orleans Item*. After serving in the Air Force during World War II, he attended the Chicago Academy of Fine Arts in Chicago, Illinois. Before switching to commercial illustration, Mr. Dobson won the Grand Prix in portrait painting from the Palette and Chisel Club. In addition to his commercial work, Steven taught illustration at the Chicago Academy of Fine Arts and night school classes at LaGrange High School. In 1987, he moved to Englewood, Florida, where he says "I am doing something that I have wanted to do all of my 'art life,' painting interesting and historic people."